The W

The car had a flat tire.

"We will put the spare wheel on the car," said Dad to Mom.

They took off the wheel
with the flat tire
and put on the spare wheel.

The wheel with the flat tire
rolled away by itself.

"Stop!" shouted Mom,
but the wheel rolled down the hill.

"Stop!" shouted Dad,
and he ran after it.

The wheel went faster.

"Stop! Stop! Stop!"
shouted the children.

The wheel hit a post.
It hit a car and a bus.

6

Then the wheel
with the flat tire
rolled into a garage
and stopped.

"Clever wheel!"
said the children.

8